By Linda Ashman

Illustrated

STELLA, UNLEASHED
Notes from the Doghouse

SCHOLASTIC INC.
New York Toronto London Auckland
Sydney Mexico City New Delhi Hong Kong

Special thanks to the dedicated volunteers and staff at shelters and rescue organizations around the country for their compassion and tireless efforts on behalf of so many animals. And endless gratitude to the Los Angeles SPCA for Remy, and Retriever Rescue of Colorado for Sammy. —Linda Ashman

No part of this publication may be reproduced, stored in a retrieval system, or transmitted in any form or by any means, electronic, mechanical, photocopying, recording, or otherwise, without written permission of the publisher. For information regarding permission, write to Sterling Publishing Co., Inc., 387 Park Avenue South, New York, NY 10016.

ISBN 978-0-545-34061-8

Text copyright © 2008 by Linda Ashman. Illustrations copyright © 2008 by Paul Meisel. All rights reserved. Published by Scholastic Inc., 557 Broadway, New York, NY 10012, by arrangement with Sterling Publishing Co., Inc. SCHOLASTIC and associated logos are trademarks and/or registered trademarks of Scholastic Inc.

12 11 10 9 8 7 6 5 4 3 2 1   11 12 13 14 15 16/0

Printed in the U.S.A.   08

First Scholastic printing, January 2011

The artwork was prepared using acrylic, gouache and pencil on Arches paper.
Designed by Lauren Rille

For Jack and Jackson and,
of course, Nicky —L. A.

For anyone who has rescued
a homeless dog —P. M.

CONTENTS

Trouble!

Out & About

The Neighborhood Pack

Final Notes

LOST & FOUND

Metal bars.
A cold, hard floor.
No window seat.
No doggy door.

Countless strangers came to call—
I listened,
watched,
and sniffed them all . . .

then turned away
and curled up tight.
Nice enough, but not quite right.

Then, one day, I sniffed a sniff
and got the most delightful whiff:
dirt and candy, grass and cake.
I stuck my paw out for a shake.

A boy knelt down.
I licked his face.
He rubbed my head.
I'd found my place.

That's how I chose this family.
Not perfect, no.

Except for me.

Binky

Fluff

WHAT'S IN A NAME?

Binky, Mitzi, Fluff, and Fritzi
sounded just plain dumb.
They hollered, "Here, Penelope!"
but I refused to come.

Fritzi

I yawned at Furby, Franci, Fifi,
BooBoo, Blanche, and Bella.
Groaned at Arfy, Pansy, Pal,
and then I heard, "Here, Stella!"

Pansy

Stella!
What a lovely name.
Simple. Stylish. Swell.
A name with heart and dignity—
it suits me very well.

Stella

BooBoo

MY BEST BUDDY

Likes to splash in puddles.
Loves to roll in dirt.
Doesn't mind some dog hair
on his lollipop or shirt.

Builds a cozy fort.
Great at playing chase.
Always shares his pillow.
Lets me kiss his face.

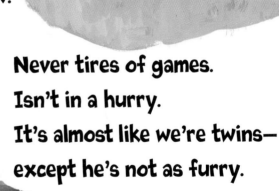

Never tires of games.
Isn't in a hurry.
It's almost like we're twins—
except he's not as furry.

THE DRAMA QUEEN

She's the doctor.
I'm the patient,
bandaged up in bed.

She's the mommy.
I'm the baby,
bonnet on my head.

This morning, it's a cowboy hat.
This afternoon, a crown.
Sometimes I'm a pirate;
other times, a clown.

She never has me fetch a stick,
or catch a rubber ball.
I wish she'd see that I'm a dog,
and not a dress-up doll.

ABOUT THIS BABY

Strange little creature.
Interesting scent.
No bark, but it surely can wail.

Not very toothy.
Frequently drools.
Cannot be trusted near tail.

Speedy on four legs.
Wobbly on two.
Often seen traveling with bear.

Splashes my water.
Plays with my toys.
Best when confined to its chair.

MOM & DAD

I drop the ball right at his feet.
It's clear I want to play.
I bark and drop it three more times.
He turns and walks away.

I whimper here beside the door.
Translation: "Let me out!"
She murmurs, "What a sweetie-dog,"
and pats me on the snout.

I stare intently at my bowl.
The message: "Fill it up."
He seems confused by my request
and fills his coffee cup.

So much I'd like to talk about:

History!
Science!
Art!

But based on observation,
it appears they're not that smart.

13

ACROBAT CAT

I do
admire this
about the cat:
She's acrobatic.

If I
could walk
on tabletops like that,
I'd be ecstatic.

14

POOR FISH

His world is that fishbowl.
Can't come out to play.
Swimming is great,
but all day, every day?

His food's worse than kibble.
His toys don't look fun.
But saddest of all,
he can't hug anyone.

MOUSE MISERY

When stuck in a cage, it's good to keep busy. But watching him run is making me dizzy.

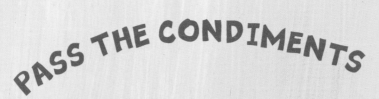

PASS THE CONDIMENTS

I am, of course,
a grateful sort,
who doesn't like to quibble.

But, really, friend,
do you intend
to feed me only kibble?

You can't deny
it's hard and dry—
just try a little nibble.

Well, I can't eat it, either.
Please—
won't you add some grated cheese?

SLEEPING REQUIREMENTS

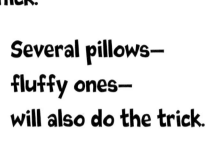

A folded blanket on the floor
is fine—
IF it is thick.

Several pillows—
fluffy ones—
will also do the trick.

A velvet couch is lovely,
if permitted,
and if not—

a sheepskin rug
is cozy
when it's in a sunny spot.

But for a truly peaceful rest,
be advised:
Your bed is best.

STELLA WIGS

STELLA FURniture

FUR EMPORIUM

You vacuum up
the clumps of hair
with obvious distaste.
You toss more in the garbage—
what a monumental waste!

Why not stuff some pillows?
Make cushions for a chair.
Create some stylish wigs for those
who need some extra hair.

Just think of all the uses—
enough to fill a store!
See, I've left another clump,
and still there's plenty more!

THE THINGS I LOVE

Walks and **treats** and belly rubs.
Drinking from a hose.
Balls and **treats** and squeaky toys.
Kisses on my nose.

Car rides with the window down.
treats, a scratch, a run.
Frisbees, **treats**, an open field.
Sleeping in the sun.

Grass and **treats** and chasing cats.
Beds with downy sheets.
Being next to you, of course.

Oh! Did I mention **treats?**

TEA TIME

This dress is not my color.
I do not like this veil.
This lace is very itchy.
Please—no ribbons on my tail!

This get-up is ungainly.
Still, I endure my fate.
After all, the scones are tasty.
Would you kindly pass the plate?

WATER!

I swim in the ocean,
no matter how rough.
In rivers and lakes—
I can't get enough!

When I see a pool,
I dive like a sub.
I **LOVE** the water—
but not in the tub.

Toto and Lassie are great, I agree.
Shiloh's got talent, but still . . .
why not me?

I can play goofy, or charming, or wild—
capture the bad guy; rescue the child;
fight off a bear on a camping vacation,
paint on some spots, I'll play a Dalmatian!

I can just see it: my face on the screen.
Gracing the cover of WOOF magazine.
Lavish hotel rooms; big, fancy cars;
strolling red carpets and sniffing the stars!

It's time to pursue my fondest ambition.
I'm off to L.A. for a movie audition—soon.
               Very soon.
But, first, a short nap.
(It's awfully cozy right here on your lap.)

23

DON'T BLAME ME!

You placed the steak on the table's edge,
then walked out of the room.
There's no one here except for me.
What else would I assume?

24

THE (almost) PERFECT HOST

I welcome guests with friendliness
(unlike the snooty cat).
Trouble is, I greet so well,
I sometimes knock them flat.

IN THE DOGHOUSE

I lunged while we were walking.
I didn't think you'd trip.
I tugged the curtain just for fun.
Who knew the thing would rip?

I knocked the knick-knacks with my tail.
Is happiness a crime?
I helped myself to a little snack.
YOU do it all the time!

I barked and woke the baby.
I dug a hole T H I S   W I D E.
I promise I'll be better.
Can I please come back inside?

STELLA

PRIZE POODLE

Mr. Fitz came over
with his poodle, Princess Kate.
She spurned the treat we offered her
(I devoured eight).

She did not drool or scratch herself.
She stood when he said, "Stand."
She sat and stayed and (worst of all)
she piddled on command.

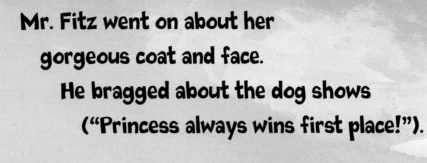

Mr. Fitz went on about her
gorgeous coat and face.
He bragged about the dog shows
("Princess always wins first place!").

Between his sickening blabber
and an extra treat or two,
I started feeling queasy,
and I threw up on his shoe.

HOWL!

I do not mind these ragged claws.
I like the dirt between my paws.
My dandruff isn't troublesome.
I'm naturally perfumed.

There's nothing wrong with matted hair.
I shed a bit, but I don't care.
Do you forget my origins?
A wolf does **NOT** get groomed.

Arrooooooooo

THE BOW-WOW BOUTIQUE

I suppose I'd wear that collar
(without the rhinestones, please).
I'll tolerate the perfume,
though it's bound to make me sneeze.

But buy that "darling" sweater
with the bows and sparkly threads—
I'll roll it in the compost pile,
then tear the thing to shreds.

VIVE LA FRANCE!

In France, I'd be welcome at shops and hotels,
indulged and adored like a queen.
I'd sit at the table in fine restaurants,
and dine on exquisite cuisine.

In France, I'd be nibbling croissants next to you.
I would not be tied to this bench.
If things do not change, I'm off to Paree—
as soon as I learn to speak French.

TWO SCOOPS, PLEASE

Vanilla is delicious, yes.
But could I ask a favor?
Next time we're at the ice-cream store,
let's try the liver flavor.

DISPATCH FROM THE FRONT LAWNS

Spike was digging holes again.
Winnie woke up late.
Uh-oh! Bruno's on the loose
(they haven't fixed that gate).

Mugsy stomped the daffodils.
Lulu lost her shoes.
Quit pulling, please!
I need some time
to sniff the latest news.

FOR BUTCH,
WHO WENT OFF TO OBEDIENCE SCHOOL

They wanted a compliant dog
who wouldn't drool or shed,
who'd lie contented at their feet
(instead of on their bed),
who'd never track in dirt or mud,
who'd do just as they wish,
who wouldn't dig or chew or snore . . .

they should have bought a fish.

AT THE DOG PARK

Sniff.
Scratch.
Dance.
Catch.
Tumble.
Wrestle.
Roll.
Run around in circles.
Dig a little hole.

Leap.
Race.
Splash.
Chase.
Hunt.
Howl.
Roam.
Boy, am I exhausted.
Could you carry me back home?

SOMEONE FOR EACH OF US

Tall and stately.

Short and stubby.

Brindled, spotted, speckled, shaggy.

Small and perky.

Large and bulky.

Wiry, curly, droopy, saggy.

Sporty, active.

Rough and tumble.

Moody types inclined to brood.

Pampered sorts

who crave attention.

Loners who need solitude.

Humans come in many forms—
different styles, sizes, traits.
Life is sweet,
and much less lonely,
when we find our perfect mates.

AT YOUR SERVICE

Alarm clock
Vacuum
Foot-warmer
Guard
Inspector of the Kitchen
Ruler of the Yard

Doorbell
Jester
Teammate
Doll
Protector of the House
Retriever of the Ball

Quick to give comfort
Slow to offend
Keeper of secrets
Friend to the end